LIVING HISTORY

BOOK THREE

by

RAY MITCHELL
and **GEOFFREY MIDDLETON**

illustrated by STUART BARRIE

HOLMES McDOUGALL LIMITED
30 ROYAL TERRACE, EDINBURGH 7

CONTENTS

CONTENTS

NOTE TO THE PUPIL

In Books I and II of LIVING HISTORY you read how people lived in Britain from early times until the end of the Middle Ages.

Book III tells how people lived and worked in town and country in Tudor and Stuart times, between the years 1485 and 1714.

This was the time of some of our famous kings and queens—Henry VIII, Elizabeth I, Charles I and Charles II. It was also the time of Drake, Raleigh, Shakespeare, Milton and Christopher Wren. It was a time of exploration and discovery, adventure on the high seas, the Plague and the Great Fire of London.

You will read about the changes that were taking place—the new houses, furniture, clothes, foods and weapons. You will read how people amused themselves, how they travelled both on land and sea, and how they earned their living.

If you keep your eyes open, you will find many of the things you read about, for history is all around you if you look for it. You may find old farmhouses or mansions near where you live. If so, try to find out if they were built in Tudor, Elizabethan or Stuart times. Visit your local museums and make drawings and notes of what you find there. Collect postcards, guide-books and photographs.

We have suggested some things for you to do—models to make, pictures to draw and paint, plays to write and act. We hope you will find out all you can about this exciting period of history and show your discoveries in as many ways as possible—in your history album, on your classroom walls, and on your history table.

Unit One

TUDOR AND STUART KINGS AND QUEENS

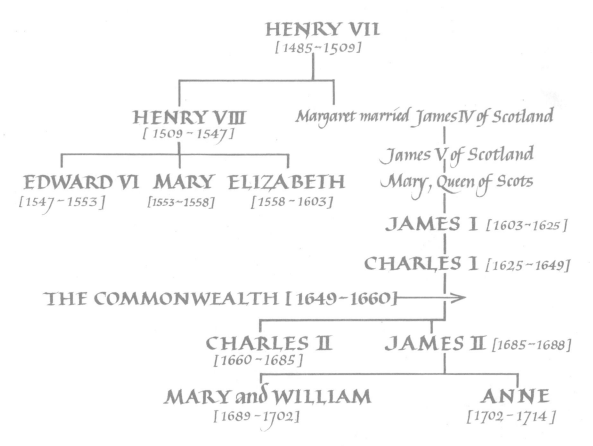

HENRY VII
[1485~1509]

HENRY VIII
[1509~1547]

Margaret married James IV of Scotland

James V of Scotland

Mary, Queen of Scots

EDWARD VI
[1547~1553]

MARY
[1553~1558]

ELIZABETH
[1558~1603]

JAMES I [1603~1625]

CHARLES I [1625~1649]

THE COMMONWEALTH [1649~1660]

CHARLES II
[1660~1685]

JAMES II [1685~1688]

MARY and WILLIAM
[1689~1702]

ANNE
[1702~1714]

The Tudor Rose

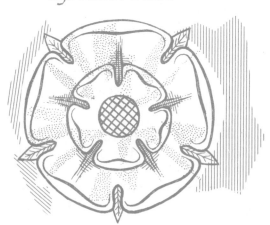

The Stuart Royal Coat-of-Arms

HENRY VII (1485 - 1509)

In 1485 the Wars of the Roses ended. Richard III was killed at the Battle of Bosworth Field and Henry Tudor was crowned king. He was the first of the Tudor kings and queens who ruled England for the next 118 years.

Henry married Elizabeth of York and joined together the two families of York and Lancaster which had fought each other for many years.

He kept the nobles in order and stopped them from keeping their own private armies. He encouraged trade and ship-building. During his reign John Cabot discovered Newfoundland.

He married his eldest son, Arthur, to a Spanish princess, Catherine of Aragon, and his daughter, Margaret, to James IV of Scotland.

When he died in 1509, England was once again peaceful and prosperous.

Henry VII

Henry VIII

HENRY VIII (1509 - 1547)

After Henry VII's death, his son, Henry VIII, became king.

In the past the church in England had always been a Catholic church with the Pope as its Head. But at this time some people, called Protestants, wanted to change or reform some of the customs and services.

In 1521 Henry wrote a book attacking the reformers. For this the Pope gave him the title of 'Defender of the Faith'. This is shown on some of our coins by the letters FID. DEF. or F.D.

Later, however, Henry quarrelled with the Pope and made himself Head of the Church in England. He also closed the monasteries because he knew the monks would obey the Pope before him. Their gold and silver plate was taken to his Treasury and their lands sold. The lead was stripped off the roofs and the buildings fell into ruins.

EDWARD VI (1547 - 1553)

Edward was king for six years and died when he was only sixteen.

Edward was a Protestant. During his reign the prayer book was re-written in English, instead of Latin. Saints, rich ornaments and some stained glass windows were removed from the churches, and wall paintings were white-washed over.

MARY (1553 - 1558)

Edward's sister, Mary, was a Catholic. She brought back Latin services and during her reign about 300 Protestants were burned at the stake. She died in 1558, hated by many of her people.

ELIZABETH I (1558 - 1603)

Elizabeth I was a popular queen who ruled England wisely and firmly for forty-five years.

Under her rule, Catholics and Protestants could live together in peace. However, from time to time, some of the Catholics plotted to put her cousin, Mary, Queen of Scots, on the English throne. Mary had fled to England when the Scottish nobles rebelled against her. Elizabeth protected her, but kept her in custody for nearly twenty years. Finally, in 1588, Elizabeth had to agree to Mary's execution after another plot was discovered.

Elizabeth I

Elizabeth's reign was a time of great exploration and discovery. One of her sailors, Sir Francis Drake, was the first Englishman to sail round the world.

JAMES I (1603 - 1625)

James I, the new King of England, was the son of Mary Stuart, Queen of Scots. He was already King of Scotland, so England and Scotland now had the same ruler, though they were governed separately. To mark the event, the cross of St. Andrew was added to that of St. George on the nation's flag.

In 1605, some of James's enemies planned to kill him when he opened Parliament, but their plot, known as the Gunpowder Plot, was discovered.

A new translation of the Bible, called the Authorised Version, was published in 1611 and is still used today.

In 1620, the Pilgrim Fathers sailed to America in the Mayflower and settled there, because in England they were not allowed to worship God in the way they wished.

Charles I

CHARLES I (1625 - 1649)

Charles I was the son of James I. He quarrelled frequently with his parliaments and ruled for 11 years without one.

The King's friends, the Royalists, were called Cavaliers. Those who supported Parliament were known as Roundheads because some wore their hair cut short, like the Puritans.

Civil war broke out between the Roundheads and the Cavaliers. The leader of the Roundheads was called Oliver Cromwell.

After many skirmishes and battles, some won by the Cavaliers and others by the Roundheads, the Royalists were defeated and Charles was taken prisoner. Later he was brought to trial at Westminster Hall and sentenced to death as a traitor.

On 30th January, 1649, King Charles climbed the scaffold outside his palace in Whitehall and was publicly executed.

James I

Oliver Cromwell

Charles II

CHARLES II (1660 - 1685)

During the reign of Charles II the Puritans were persecuted. Many fled to America and others were thrown into prison. John Bunyan spent 12 years in Bedford Prison and while there he wrote ' The Pilgrim's Progress '.

The Plague and the Great Fire of London occurred during Charles's reign.

JAMES II (1685 - 1688)

James II, the brother of Charles II, tried to make England a Roman Catholic country.

The Duke of Monmouth led a rebellion against James, but was defeated. Judge Jeffreys sentenced over 300 of the rebels to a cruel death and sent many more to the West Indies as slaves.

Parliament invited James's daughter, Mary, and her husband, William of Orange, to take the throne of England. William landed at Torbay and James fled to France.

THE COMMONWEALTH (1649 - 1660)

After Charles's death England had no king and became a republic. Oliver Cromwell was the real ruler of the country and was called Lord Protector of the Commonwealth.

Under his rule the Puritans destroyed statues, carvings and paintings in the churches. Dancing, bear-baiting and acting were all considered sinful by the Puritans and were forbidden.

After Cromwell's death, Prince Charles was invited to return from Holland to become king.

James II

William & Mary
1689-1702

Anne
1702-1714

WILLIAM AND MARY (1689 - 1702)

William and Mary ruled together as King and Queen until Mary died in 1694. During their reign, Parliament became more powerful and all Protestants were free to worship as they wished.

After Mary's death in 1694, William ruled by himself until he died in 1702. Mary's sister, Anne, then became Queen.

ANNE (1702 - 1714)

Anne was the last of the Stuart rulers. During her reign the English army, commanded by John Churchill, Duke of Marlborough, defeated the French.

After 1707, under the Treaty of Union, England and Scotland were governed by the same parliament and used the same coinage, weights and measures.

The Battle of Blenheim was Marlborough's greatest victory over the French

10

SOME THINGS TO DO

Mary Queen of Scots

1. Paint large pictures of the Tudor Rose and the Stuart Royal Coat-of-Arms.

2. The Pope gave Henry VIII the title of ' Defender of the Faith.'
   Make ' rubbings ' of the coins which bear the letters F.D. or FID. DEF. Lay the coins on your desk, place a piece of paper on top and pencil over the coins.

3. Find out from your reference books all you can about Mary, Queen of Scots. Imagine you are living in the year 1588 and Mary has just been executed. Write a letter to a friend telling the story of Mary's life.

4. Write sentences about:—
   a. Two things that Henry VIII did during his reign;
   b. Henry VIII and the monasteries;
   c. What happened to the churches during the reign of Edward VI.

5. Draw a flag to show the crosses of St. Andrew and St. George. Colour it.

6. Find a book which tells you the story of Guy Fawkes. Write a play about it with the following scenes:
   i. A plot is hatched to blow up the Houses of Parliament. Guy Fawkes is chosen to do it.
   ii. One of the plotters warns his friend in a letter.
   iii. A message is received by the King.
   iv. Soldiers discover Guy Fawkes in the cellar.

7. Trace these figures on to cardboard, cut them out and colour them. Stand them up on slotted corks.

Cavalier Roundhead

FARMING

Strip Fields

At the beginning of Tudor times, most of the people still lived in the countryside and farmed their land in the way that their fore-fathers had done in the Middle Ages.

In some places the farmers had their own fields with hedges or fences round them, and these men were free to grow whatever crops they needed.

In many other places, however, the farmers still lived in open-field villages, where they all grew their crops together in the large, open fields round the village.

The fields were divided into strips and each farmer had a number of strips in each field. He had a share of the hay from the meadow and he grazed his cattle on the heath or common land.

All the strips had to be ploughed, sown and harvested at the same time and all the farmers had to grow the same crops. This was not always a good way of farming, as we shall see later.

Money Rents

In the past the open-field farmers had paid for their strips by working for the lord of the manor who owned the land. They had to work for him on two or three days a week and at the busy times of the year. They could not leave the village without his permission and there were many other things they had to do for him. So they were not free men.

However, as time passed, these customs had slowly changed and by Tudor times many of the farmers were paying the lord a money rent instead of working for him. By the end of Queen Elizabeth's reign all men were free.

Paying money rent to the Lord

Other Changes

In the past the villagers had been happy if they had enough crops to feed their own families. But by now the towns were becoming larger and many of the townsfolk were too busy in other trades to grow all their own food. So if a farmer had more food than he needed for himself, he could sell the extra crops for money in the town market. Then he was able to buy more comforts for his home or rent more land from the lord.

This made some of the farmers want to grow more crops and they began to think of better ways of farming. In the open fields their crops were sometimes spoilt by weeds from their neighbour's strips or by cattle straying into the fields. Time was wasted by having to move from one strip to another, and they could not grow the crops they wanted unless all the other

Tudor Farm House

farmers agreed. So some exchanged strips with their neighbours and gathered their land together in one block to make a field.

Other farmers made new fields out of the heathland, cleared the edges of woods, and drained marshes.

Sometimes they rented new fields which the lord made from parts of the waste land which had not been previously used.

Then the farmers put hedges and fences round the fields to keep out stray cattle, and dug ditches to drain the land.

Now that they had their own fields, they were able to farm the land in the way they wished.

Those who earned more money rented more land from the lord or took over other strips from the poorer farmers. They hired men to work for them and built new and better houses.

Farmer and wife riding to market

However, while some of the farmers grew richer, many of the villagers became poorer.

For a long time English wool had been the best in Europe. It was in great demand and fetched a high price. Sheep farmers and wool merchants became very wealthy, so landowners and the larger farmers turned more of their land into sheep-runs instead of growing crops.

When this happened, there was less work for the villagers. Only a shepherd and his dogs were needed to look after sheep. The other labourers had to find work elsewhere.

At this time, too, some of the landlords fenced off parts of the common land to make more sheep-runs. The villagers' cattle were driven off and had nowhere to graze. As a result the villagers had less food.

Prices were rising and it cost more to buy things. People needed more money. Many of the landlords raised the rents or asked for more money when a son took over his father's land. Those who could not pay were turned off their land and sometimes their houses were pulled down.

Lord's men pulling down a cottage

After Henry VIII closed the monasteries, there was no one to help the poor. Some went to the towns to find work there. However, many wandered from place to place. No one wanted them. Some became beggars and thieves and, if caught, they were whipped, branded or put in the stocks.

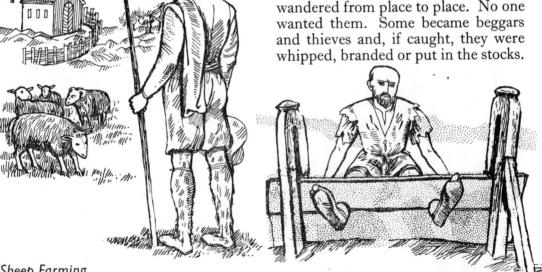

Sheep Farming

Beggar in the stocks

Ploughing, sowing and harrowing,

By the time of Queen Elizabeth, there were so many beggars and ruffians wandering about the country that something had to be done. So Elizabeth passed laws which said that the poor must be sent back to the village where they were born. Each parish had to collect money, called a ' poor rate ', to care for them and to give them work.

By now, too, there was so much wool that the price had fallen. So many landowners and farmers ploughed up their sheep-runs and began to grow crops again. More workers were needed, villages began to prosper, and new houses were built.

For many years yet, however, through the reigns of Elizabeth and the Stuarts, the old ways of farming still continued.

Although some farmers had fields with hedges or fences round them, many still grew their crops in the open fields. Part of the land was left fallow each year and did not produce crops. Seed was still sown by hand and so much of it was wasted.

A few farmers were beginning to try new crops, such as clover and turnips, to feed the cattle during the winter when the grass didn't grow. But most of the cattle still had to be slaughtered in the autumn because there was not enough food to keep them alive throughout the winter. The meat was salted or pickled to last until the spring.

The cattle and sheep were much smaller and thinner than those of today.

The main crops of those days were barley, rye and wheat. When the seed was sown, the children were sent to the fields to scare away the birds.

At harvest-time the corn was cut with sickles and threshed with flails. A flail was two pieces of wood joined together by a piece of leather. The corn was thrown on the ground and hit with the flail to separate the chaff from the grain.

The most important man in the village was now the 'squire'. Sometimes he came from the family which had once been the lords of the manor. But often he was a merchant or business man who had become wealthy through trade, bought land and decided to live in the country. He was usually the Justice of the Peace and it was his duty to see that the villagers obeyed the laws. He punished anyone who did not do so.

The larger farms were worked by 'yeomen' farmers. Some owned their land and others paid a money rent. As well as working on the land, their

Threshing and winnowing

families earned money by spinning wool, weaving cloth, and making baskets and gloves at home. Many of the villagers worked on the farms for wages, but each village also had its craftsmen, such as blacksmiths, carpenters and wheelwrights, millers and bakers.

Scaring birds

Blacksmith

SOME THINGS TO DO

1. You are the son of a farmer during Tudor times. Your father wants to grow more crops to sell in the town market.

   Make up a story about what he did. Tell how he exchanged strips with his neighbours—made a new field on the edge of the woods—kept out the cattle and drained the land.

   Some years later your father died. Tell the story of what happened when you went to the landlord for permission to take over your father's land.

2. Paint large pictures of:—

   i. A farmer making a new field on the edge of a wood.

   ii. Two men standing in a strip field pointing at the strips and exchanging land.

   iii. Men pulling down a village cottage.

   iv. A farmer riding to market on horseback.

   v. Men driving cattle out of a field which is being fenced.

   vi. A shepherd and his dog looking after sheep.

   vii. A beggar being whipped while another is being put in the stocks.

   viii. Men working in the fields, ploughing and sowing.

   ix. Men threshing corn.

   Paste each picture on to a large sheet of stiff paper, make them into a book and call it 'Our Book about Tudor Farming.'

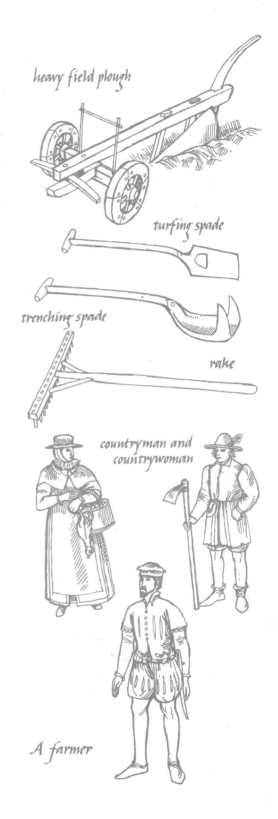

heavy field plough

turfing spade

trenching spade

rake

countryman and countrywoman

A farmer

17

COTTAGES AND FARMHOUSES

Village Cottages

There were no proper streets or roads, but only rough tracks through the village. The cottages were still scattered around the church as they had been in the Middle Ages. Some faced one way and some another. Each had its own small plot of land where the family grew vegetables and herbs.

Some were the old 'cruck' type of house and others had a timber frame with wattle and daub walls.

Many of the houses had only one room. This was used for cooking, eating, sleeping and all the jobs that had to be done indoors.

Sometimes there was a small bedroom in a loft at one end with a ladder to reach it. Or there might be a small room built on the side of the house.

All the houses had earth floors with the fire in the middle of the room, and the smoke escaped through a hole in the roof.

There were few windows and no glass in them. Rough wooden shutters kept out the wind and the rain.

Interior

There was very little furniture—just a plank or trestle table, a few stools, and flock or straw mattresses. People slept on the floor with sacks or rags to keep them warm.

Timber framed cottage with "outshut"

Cruck House

Farmhouses

The farmers who had become more prosperous wanted larger and more comfortable homes, with proper bedrooms upstairs. So they built new farmhouses outside the village, near their fields.

Some were built of stone, but most of them had a timber framework with wattle and daub walls or lath and plaster.

To avoid the danger of fire, cooking was still done in the middle of the room, and a hole had to be left in the roof for the smoke to escape. So the main room, which was used both as the kitchen and living room, was like a small hall, open to the rafters.

The bedrooms were built at the end of the hall, over the parlour or the pantry, in a two-storey building.

Later, the fire was moved to a huge brick fireplace and chimney stack at one end of the hall. Then beams were put across the hall to make another bedroom upstairs.

Yeoman's timber framed house, "jettied"

Chimney on end

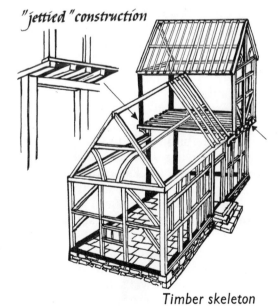

"jettied" construction

Timber skeleton

Timber house at Abbotts Bromley, Staffs.

cut-away view of spiral staircase & fireplace

At first the bedroom floor jutted out beyond the ground floor, like a 'jetty'. This was because the carpenters laid the joists flat, instead of upright as we do today. To stop the bedroom floor from moving up and down when people walked over it, they had to use longer planks and build the bedroom walls on the ends. Then the weight of the walls kept the floor firm and steady.

However, by the time of Queen Elizabeth the carpenters had learned how to build high straight walls without using 'jetties' and to build brick chimney stacks inside the houses.

Then people could have fires in each room and a wooden spiral staircase by the side of the chimney stack instead of a ladder to go upstairs.

When bricks were cheaper, some of the people with 'jettied' houses re-built the lower walls in brick so that the front of the house was straight and flat.

Then they, too, could have a central chimney stack and staircase.

Hundreds of two-storey farmhouses and small cottages were built in the country during the sixteenth century and we can still see many of them today.

Jettied house with rebuilt lower walls

MANOR HOUSES AND MANSIONS

During Tudor times, some of the lords and landowners became rich after taking over lands which had belonged to the monasteries.

Many of them built new timber manor houses, with tile or thatch roofs, while others used stone.

A new material was also being used. Bricks were being brought here from Flanders in the boats which came to collect the English wool, and so brick houses began to appear in some parts of the country.

Some of the new houses were built round courtyards to give more rooms.

At the entrance to the courtyard was a tall gatehouse.

Round the sides were rooms or 'lodgings' for guests and servants and at the far end was the great hall.

This had a fine timber roof, carved screens, a raised dais and a beautiful bay window. At one end was a parlour or separate dining room where the family ate their meals in private, away from the servants. Over the parlour was the main bedroom.

Gatehouse

Tudor timber Manor house, Ockwells, Berks.

A	Great Hall	E	Kitchen
B	Dais	F	Servants' Hall
C	Library	G	Parlour
D	Gatehouse	H	Lodgings

Plan of Tudor Mansion

Horham Hall, Essex

Montacute House, Somerset.

Many more new mansions were built in the reign of Queen Elizabeth. By then the house was a long building, with a block or 'wing' of rooms at each end. Built in red brick or stone, it was often three storeys high. In front was a terrace, with a flight of stone steps down to the gardens.

On the roof were curved gables and tall chimney stacks.

By now, the main door had been moved to the centre of the front, and the windows were arranged on each side so that they matched or balanced each other.

Both Tudor and Elizabethan mansions were 'full of windows'. Large bays stretched from floor to ceiling, sometimes two storeys high. Some, called 'oriels', jutted out from an upper floor.

The windows were filled with small panes of glass, held together with lead strips. Some sections were fastened on hinges, so they opened like doors. These are called 'casement' windows.

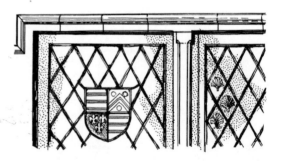

Lead latticed windows

22

Both Tudors and Elizabethans were very fond of flowers and grew them both for their perfume and their colour.

Each large house had gardens with green lawns, straight paths and flower beds arranged in squares, rectangles, triangles and circles. The beds were edged with box or lavender bushes or low stone walls.

Yew and privet bushes were cut and trimmed to look like birds and animals. Here and there about the gardens and lawns were fountains and statues, and sometimes a sundial.

Many different kinds of herbs were grown to flavour food and make ointments and medicines.

Each house had a vegetable garden and an orchard. There were apples,

Plan of a maze

pears, plums, peaches, apricots, figs, mulberries and strawberries. Red and black currants were grown and walnuts, almonds and filberts.

Many of the large houses had a maze, and finding their way out of it was a favourite pastime for adults as well as children.

Tudor Garden

23

Elizabethan hall

The wealthy Tudor and Elizabethan lords often entertained their friends and relations, and sometimes the Queen and her attendants. So, as well as the hall, there were sitting rooms or parlours, bedrooms, a large dining room, kitchens, larders, pantries and store-rooms.

Their houses were much more comfortable than the old stone castles of the Middle Ages, and were full of colour and decoration.

Walls were panelled in oak or covered with painted cloths and tapestries.

Ceilings were plastered and decorated with patterns. Figures of flowers, fruit, animals and monograms were moulded in the plaster.

Floors were covered with stone slabs or boarded with oak planks.

Rushes and sweet-smelling herbs were scattered over them.

Each of the main rooms had a wall fireplace, where logs blazed on iron ' dogs ' under a carved mantelpiece.

Carved wooden over-mantel

24

Oak staircases, with carved balustrades, led to the bedrooms on the upper floors.

There was little furniture in the bedrooms, and clothes were usually kept in a long chest. There was a basin and jug for washing, and a metal mirror.

The main rooms had large four-poster beds. This kind of bed had a wooden roof and back. At night curtains were drawn round it to keep out the draughts, so it was like a small room inside a room.

On the bed was a wool or feather mattress, which rested on wooden boards or on ropes stretched across the framework. Over this were linen sheets, woollen blankets and a quilt.

Children often slept in the same room on trundle or truckle beds.

16th century staircase

These were like small boxes on wheels, so they could be pushed under the four-poster beds.

People usually slept in their shirts or chemises and wore nightcaps.

Elizabethan bedroom

Long gallery

On one of the upper floors there was often a long, narrow room, which stretched across the house. This was the 'long gallery', where the family and their guests amused themselves with music, games and dancing, and where they walked for exercise in bad weather.

Downstairs, in the kitchens, meat was roasted on spits, turned by wheels or pulleys.

Sometimes the spits were turned by a small dog in a cage on the wall. As he walked, he turned the cage and this worked the pulleys and the spits. The bread was baked in a wall-oven in the chimney corner.

16th century kitchen

SOME THINGS TO DO

1. Make a model of the Tudor farm-house shown on page 19.

    First build the framework from strips of wood. Remember that the upper floor jutted out beyond the ground floor.

    Fill the spaces between the timbers with clay or plaster. Leave gaps for the doors and windows.

    Thatch the roof with straw or reeds.

2. Paint a large wall-picture to show the different kinds of cottages and farmhouses.

    Label the hall, parlour, pantry-kitchen and bedrooms.

3. Paint a picture of the interior of a village cottage showing father bringing in vegetables, mother cooking, young children playing on the floor and older brothers and sisters having their meal at the table.

4. Draw a plan of a Tudor mansion built around a courtyard.

    Label the hall, parlour, kitchen, lodgings and gatehouse.

5. Find out if there is a Tudor mansion or farmhouse in your district. If so, try to get permission to visit it. Take your notebook and pencil with you. Make sketches of the outside, the chimneys, doors and windows.

    Write notes about your visit when you return to school.

East Anglian farm houses of the period

6. Make a book about houses in Tudor times. Call it 'My Book of Tudor Houses.' Your Contents page could include these:—

      Village Cottages,
      Farmhouses,
      Manor Houses,
      Mansions.

Show mother cooking at the fire in the middle of the room, a young boy asleep on the floor in the corner and other members of the family eating at a rough trestle table. (Page 18 will help you.)

On the right-hand page write about your picture.

Write the other chapters of your book in the same way, but remember that in some chapters you will need more pages. For example, an *ELIZABETHAN MANSION* will need pages for:—

a. The outside of the house,
b. The Gardens,
c. The Bedroom,
d. The Hall and Staircase,
e. The Long Gallery,
f. The Kitchen,
g. The Parlour.

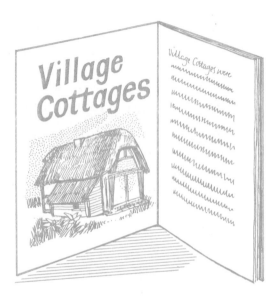

You could start like this:—

Open the book at the first double page. At the top of the left-hand page write the title of your first chapter—*VILLAGE COTT-AGES.* Below this draw a large picture of a Tudor cottage.

On the right-hand page write how it was built, what it looked like and who lived in it.

Turn over to the next double page and write the heading *INSIDE THE COTTAGE* at the top of the left-hand page. Below it draw a picture of the interior of the cottage.

Tudor chimneys

LONDON

The largest town in England at the time of the Tudors and Stuarts was London. We cannot be certain of its population, for in those days few accurate records were kept. However, at the time of Queen Elizabeth we think there were about 200,000 people living there.

We do know it was a densely crowded city, for London was much smaller then than it is nowadays. Most of it was in that part of London we now call 'the City,' though it had already begun to spread to the open fields beyond its wall.

London Wall stretched from the Tower of London round three sides of the city to the Fleet Ditch, one of the streams which ran into the River Thames.

The main roads to London led through gates in the city wall. These gates were closed at nightfall.

Travellers from the North entered the city through Bishopsgate, Moorgate and Cripplegate. Those from the West came in through Ludgate or Newgate, and those from the East through Aldgate.

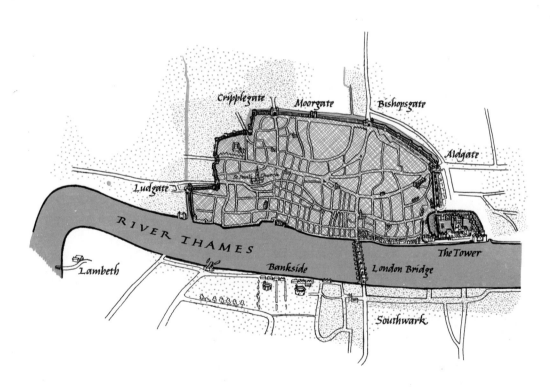

Pictorial map of 16th century London

*London Bridge, showing Bridgegate with
its row of heads*

On the fourth side of the city was the broad River Thames, which was crossed by London Bridge.

This had twenty arches, and houses and shops on both sides of the narrow roadway across the bridge. At the southern end was a drawbridge and a great gateway called the Bridgegate. Over it were poles, on which were fixed the heads of traitors who had been executed. Sometimes there were as many as thirty heads.

Usually the Thames was crowded with boats of many kinds, for it was quicker, safer and far more pleasant to travel along the river highway than it was to push through the dirty, crowded, narrow streets of the city.

People came down the steps to the riverside and called out for a waterman to take them further along the river, or across to the other side. The watermen were quarrelsome and often fought each other and sometimes even their passengers.

Merchant ships laden with cargoes from across the seas unloaded their goods at the wharves of Billingsgate.

The Queen travelled along the river too, and scarlet-clad watermen rowed the royal barge between the palaces along the river. Those at Greenwich, Hampton Court, Richmond and Windsor were in the country away from the smells and dirt of the city. The chief palace was Whitehall

Palace in Westminster, which stood where the street called Whitehall is now. Sometimes a royal court was held at St. James's Palace.

The Tower of London, too, was a royal palace, but although Queen Elizabeth I stayed there on the night before her coronation, she did not use it very often afterwards. Perhaps she remembered only too well those days when, as a young princess, she had been imprisoned behind its thick walls by her sister, Queen Mary.

The Tower was not only a palace and a fortress which guarded the city, but also a prison. Those who offended the king or queen were sent there as traitors, and few left the Tower alive. Most of them, after long imprisonment or hours of cruel torture, were taken out to Tower Hill. There they were beheaded before large crowds who assembled to watch their execution.

Execution on Tower Hill

Tower of London

There were many other fine buildings in London as well as royal palaces. Many wealthy merchants and noblemen had grand houses with lovely gardens built along the river bank, which was known as the Strand.

In the centre of the city was the large church of St. Paul's with its tall steeple. Soon after Elizabeth I became Queen, this steeple was struck by lightning, which set it on fire, and the whole church roof was burned. Although the roof was later repaired, the steeple was never replaced.

31

The church was used, not only for worship, but also as a meeting place where citizens talked and did their business. It was a crowded, noisy place.

The nave of the church was called Paul's Walk and was often like a market-place with its stalls, scribes and lawyers.

Westminster Abbey

Paul's Walk

In St. Paul's Churchyard were many booksellers' shops, and from each one hung a gaily painted sign. Outside the shops the books were displayed on trestle stalls. Behind these stood the prentices shouting their wares, each one trying to shout louder than the other. In the middle of the Churchyard was a cross where people gathered to listen to famous preachers of the day.

Not far away was the Guildhall where the Lord Mayor and Council met to govern the city. The nearby Royal Exchange was a meeting-place for merchants. Both these buildings were later destroyed in the Great Fire.

Parliament met at Westminster Hall, which was also the scene of many trials. Nearby stood Westminster Abbey, very much the same as it is to-day.

London was a city of many churches, for there were almost a hundred within the city walls. One of the most famous was St. Mary-le-Bow which had a fine peal of bells.

The Streets of London

But London was not all magnificent buildings. The crowded city was closely packed with overhanging, timbered houses and shops, huddled together in narrow streets.

Rubbish was thrown into the streets, where it rotted and stank, particularly in hot weather. There were few collectors to take it away in carts.

Although there were wells of drinking water at such places as Clerkenwell and Sadler's Wells outside the city, most people fetched their water from the Fleet Ditch or the Walbrook.

These were two streams which ran through the middle of the city and flowed into the Thames.

Carriers took round the water in buckets which hung from a yoke across their shoulders, or in a large tankard, rather like a milk-churn, which was carried on their backs.

Sometimes the water was brought from the rivers in trenches or conduits, which usually ended in public fountains. But the rivers and conduits became choked with the rubbish thrown into them, and the filthy drinking water spread diseases.

London street in the 17th century

33

L.H. 3—C

The Plague

One dreadful disease which frequently broke out was a dangerous fever called the plague. Most people died very soon after catching it for no-one knew for certain how it could be cured.

The plague spread swiftly and was probably carried from house to house by rats which swarmed among the red cross was painted on the door to warn people to keep away.

The doors were bolted and windows shuttered, and a watchman was placed outside the house to prevent anyone from entering or leaving.

People in the closed house called down from the upper windows for food to be thrown up to them. But there were too many infected houses

Plague infested houses being guarded by watchmen

filthy rubbish in the streets. The plague was usually at its worst during the hot summer months.

The worst outbreak was in the year 1665 when the plague swept rapidly throughout London. New laws were made to try to stop it from spreading, but these were not always kept. No-one was supposed to leave a house in which someone had the plague. A and not enough watchmen, and people often left their homes at night.

Sometimes they dropped things on the watchmen from above and then made their escape, spreading disease wherever they went.

Those who could not escape from the boarded-up houses faced almost certain death for the plague was very infectious.

People were terrified of catching the plague and many left the city for the cleaner air of the country. Sometimes they carried the disease with them.

At night, burial carts rumbled along the cobbled city streets to collect the dead.

So many people died that it was soon impossible to give them a decent burial because the churchyards were full. Large, deep pits were dug and the bodies were tipped from the carts into these rough mass graves. No one liked doing this unpleasant, dangerous work and the wealthier people paid large sums of money for the bodies of their loved ones to be removed from the houses.

When the plague was at its worst, thousands of people died each week.

At one stage it was feared that no-one would be left alive to bury the dead. At last, however, as the hot summer months faded, the numbers of the dead dropped slightly.

As the cold winter approached, the infectious germs did not spread so quickly and the plague began to die down.

People began to return to the city from the countryside, though it was some months before the King and his court returned to Whitehall Palace.

But gradually the shops re-opened and those who had survived the terrors of the plague walked the streets again.

Nearly 100,000 people had perished. Samuel Pepys, a famous man of that time, wrote in his diary . . . 'they tell me that in Westminster there is not one physician left alive.'

Burial cart collecting dead at night

The Thames with St. Paul's silhouetted against the Flames

The Great Fire

A few months after the plague died down, another disaster befell the city. A fire, which started in a baker's shop in Pudding Lane, spread throughout the city and grew into the worst fire England had yet known.

The closely packed timber houses were quickly destroyed by flames, fanned into a fierce blaze by a strong wind. There were no fire brigades to put out the fires, and the buckets of water which most people kept outside their houses were of little use against the raging inferno.

People dragged their furniture and other possessions from the blazing

Fire spreading from house to house

houses and carried them through the crowded streets to a place of safety. Some sought shelter in the houses of friends, only to move again as soon as the fire overtook them.

Many carried their belongings on their backs, as there were not enough carts for all to use. Some, too, could not afford the large sums of money demanded for their hire.

Large numbers took to boats and the Thames became crowded with heavily laden vessels. Even some of the houses on London Bridge were ablaze.

Orders were given for houses in the path of the fire to be pulled down in an attempt to stop its spread. This could be done quite easily by fixing long hooks to the roofs.

On most occasions the fire overtook the workers before the demolished houses could be cleared away, and the piles of dry timber and thatch only added further fuel to the flames. Others of course, did not want to pull down their homes and hoped for a miracle to save them.

After the fire had raged for four days and nights, further orders were given for the houses to be blown up by gunpowder. People were frightened when they heard the loud explosions and wondered what new horror was to befall them.

The blown-up houses left larger gaps across which the flames could not leap. So gradually the fires died down and burned themselves out, though for many weeks afterwards the smouldering timbers again burst into flames from time to time.

After the Fire

Much of the city had been destroyed and many fine buildings, including St. Paul's Cathedral, the Guildhall and the Royal Exchange, had been burned to the ground. Whole streets of shops and houses had been destroyed and thousands of people left homeless.

Houses in the path of the fire being pulled down

Fortunately, the weather was fine and they were able to camp in the fields outside the city. Many had been unable to save any of their possessions and had no money to replace them.

Some had buried money and other valuables in their gardens. When they returned later, often they could not find them because they had been stolen.

People wanted to know how the fire had started. Some thought it was a punishment from God for their sins.

Others thought it was the work of the foreigners who lived in the city. Many found it difficult to believe that it had really been started by an overheated oven in a baker's shop in Pudding Lane.

Although the Great Fire was a terrible disaster, very few people lost their lives and a large number of the dirty, plague-infested houses had been destroyed. In the years that followed, a new and cleaner city arose from the ashes of the old.

Plans were put forward for rebuilding fire-damaged London. Some people thought the city should be replanned with new wide streets, but this proved to be too costly.

Some taxes were raised by the City Council, but everyone was anxious to build his own house as soon as possible. As a result only a few streets were widened and most houses were rebuilt where they had been before.

The monument

The fire had shown people the danger of living in timber houses, so some of the new houses were built of brick and stone.

Sir Christopher Wren, a famous architect, was one whose plans for a new city were not accepted, but he designed many fine new churches. Some, such as St. Mary-le-Bow in Cheapside and St. Bride's in Fleet Street, had beautiful spires or steeples.

Wren rebuilt St. Paul's Cathedral as it is to-day, a task which took nearly forty years. From his house across the Thames he could watch the growth of this fine new cathedral.

Only a few buildings which survived the fire can still be seen to-day. Not far from St. Paul's is the Monument which stands near the spot where the Great Fire of 1666 started.

Wren's St. Paul's Cathedral

SOME THINGS TO DO

1. Make a wall-frieze of a London street at the time of Queen Elizabeth.

   Join together large sheets of paper (kitchen paper, sugar paper or newspaper) to make a long strip. Fasten this to one of your classroom walls. Then draw the houses and people on the frieze with sticks of charcoal and paint them.   *OR*

   Make separate paintings on sheets of paper, cut them out and stick them on the frieze.

2. Samuel Pepys kept a diary at the time of the Plague. Imagine you, too, lived in those days. Make up a diary for each day of a week, telling of the dreadful things you saw or heard about during the Plague.

3. Answer these questions in complete sentences.

Water carrier

a. What were the names of the main gates leading into the City of London?

b. Where did the Londoners get their water supply?

c. Why did people often travel along the Thames instead of using the streets?

4. Write some sentences about:—
   a. The Tower of London,
   b. The Strand,
   c. St. Paul's Cathedral,
   d. The streets of London,
   e. Water-carriers.

*Queen Elizabeth being rowed down river
in her royal barge*

5. Make up a play about the Great Fire of London. You can mime some of the scenes.

Scene 1. *In the bedroom.*
A family in bed—one awakes—smells smoke and hears crackling—jumps out of bed—runs to window—sees flames across narrow street—rouses rest of family.

Scene 2. *Downstairs.*
The family gather together valuable possessions—chests and other furniture moved out of room—loaded on to handcart and trundled away—other goods carried on backs.

Scene 3. *In the street.*
Men are ordered to pull down houses—use of long hooks—alarm as fire spreads—piles of thatch and timber catch alight—people run away—ordered back—some collapse and are pulled away from flames.

Scene 4. *Later.*
King Charles, his brother, and the Lord Mayor of London arrive—they help to pull down houses—the King orders houses to be blown up—men are sent for barrels of gunpowder—the barrels are put into empty houses and exploded.

Scene 5. *Moorfields—A Few Days Later.*
The King visits people who are homeless and camping out—different people tell their stories of what happened to them—the King sympathises with his people.

6. Scenes 2 and 3 of your play are illustrated on this page. Draw your own picture for Scene 4 and colour it.

7. Paint a large picture of people returning to the charred ruins of their homes. Show them searching for money and other valuables they had hidden and buried in the garden before the fire.

a) Scene 2

b) Scene 3

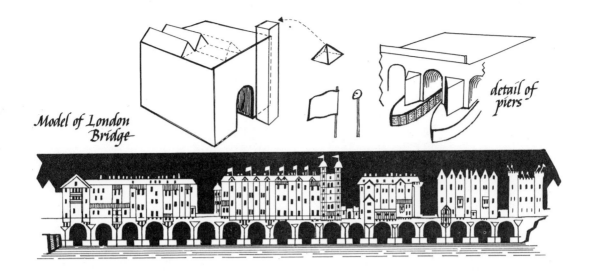

Model of London Bridge

detail of piers

8. Make a large class model of London Bridge. Use cardboard boxes to make the houses. The heads on poles can be made of clay or papier-maché fastened on pieces of dowelling.

9. You are a news reporter in the year 1666. Write an article for your newspaper about the Fire of London. Tell how the fire started, how you saw the houses blazing and people dragging furniture and possessions from their homes. Tell how you saw other people escaping down the river, and of the unsuccessful attempts made to stop the fire from spreading. Say how the fires were eventually controlled.

10. Paint a large picture for your classroom wall of the Great Fire of London. You can either show a street scene or a view of the blazing city taken from the top of Old St. Paul's.

11. Make a book about London in Tudor and Stuart times in the same way as you made your book about Tudor Houses. Remember to include a Contents page, to draw large pictures on the left-hand pages and to write about them on the right-hand pages.

You could include a chapter about Sir Christopher Wren and the buildings he designed after the Fire.

Old St Paul's Church before the Great Fire 1666

LIFE IN THE TOWNS

Although most people still lived in hamlets and villages, some of the medieval towns had grown larger. But they were still much smaller than towns are nowadays.

Apart from London, the largest town in England in Tudor times was Norwich. However, its population was only about 17,000, compared with almost 120,000 at the present time.

Leicester was an average sized town of about 4,000 people, whereas its present-day population is over 270,000.

Bristol and Plymouth were both growing ports. Other towns such as Stamford, Shrewsbury and Stratford-on-Avon were still little more than overgrown villages, with fields and woods surrounding them.

Quite a few towns were still encircled by strong walls which had been built during the Middle Ages. People entered and left the town through strong iron gates which were closed at sunset.

Other towns had spread beyond their walls or had neglected to repair them.

The streets were very narrow and were often paved with cobble-stones. There were no pavements as we know them and people had to draw back into the doorways to allow carts and coaches to pass by.

Housewives threw their rubbish into the streets and during wet weather this was churned into mud by the horses' hoofs.

Only a few of the largest towns had scavengers or dustmen to collect the rubbish which people heaped outside their doors. This was dumped into the river or outside the town walls.

Main towns of the Tudor and Stuart periods

Narrow, muddy town street

*Night traveller and linkboy. Robbers
lurking in the background*

Although most towns were near a river the water was unfit to drink. So in some of the larger towns water carriers went round the streets selling water from one of the wells.

At night the streets were dark and dangerous. They were only feebly lit by lanterns at corners or outside inns. The shadows of overhanging houses were ideal hiding-places for thieves and footpads, waiting to attack and rob any lone citizen.

Most people were home behind their bolted doors before nightfall. Those who had to journey about the streets after dark hired a link-boy to accompany them and hold a lantern or torch.

Some towns had watchmen who patrolled the streets throughout the night. But most of these men were old and feeble and kept out of the way if any trouble arose.

They carried a staff and lantern and called out the time each hour throughout the night—' Two o'clock, a frosty night and all's well!'

During the day the streets were crowded and very noisy. Many of the goods were sold by hawkers, who walked up and down the streets shouting their wares. Their loud cries mingled with the rival shouts of tinkers, basket-makers, chair-menders and other craftsmen.

Carts and wagons rattled over the cobble-stones and added to the general noise and confusion, while fierce arguments broke out concerning rights of way and prices of goods. These sometimes led to duels in the streets.

Merchants and Craftsmen

The merchant or shopkeeper lived at his place of business. His shop, which was in the front room of his

Merchant's house

house, had a large window overlooking the street, It had no glass, but large, wooden shutters were let down as a counter during the day and covered the window at night.

Behind the shop was the merchant's parlour, or office, and his kitchen, while on the floors above were other living rooms and bedrooms.

The wealthier merchants had houses of three or four storeys with warehouses behind them in which their goods were stored. Often houses by a riverside had a quay where ships' cargoes could be unloaded.

The merchant wrote letters concerning his business with a quill pen on one side of a sheet of stiff paper. There were no envelopes and the letter was folded and fastened with a blob of hot wax.

On this the merchant pressed his ring, or seal. The letter could not be opened without the wax being broken.

As there was no postal service, the letter was delivered by messenger. Sometimes a copy of the letter was sent by another messenger in case the first failed to arrive safely.

Ship unloading at merchant's quayside warehouse

44

Fight between apprentices

Apprentices

In the larger towns were all kinds of merchants and craftsmen. There were wool merchants, armourers, saddlers, goldsmiths, turners, coopers, fullers, dyers, masons, cutters, barbers, skinners and many others.

The names of these trades often became surnames, for a man first known as John the Cooper, or Tom the Saddler, was soon called John Cooper, or Tom Saddler.

Most merchants had one or more boys called apprentices who were learning the trade.

An agreement called an indenture was made between the master and the apprentice. The boy's father usually paid a sum of money, called a premium, to the merchant or craftsman.

The master agreed to feed, clothe and house the boy for seven years and to teach him his trade. In return, the boy promised to obey his master and to keep the rules made by the town council. These were often very strict, for it was feared that apprentices might join together in gangs and become a nuisance in the town.

In some towns a curfew bell was rung each night at nine o'clock, by which time the apprentice must be back at his master's house.

He was not allowed to carry a sword or dagger, but only the knife with which he cut his meat at mealtimes. Even so, there were often fights in the streets between gangs of apprentices. Occasionally they would even attack and rob the citizens.

45

Apprentice being beaten

Some were kept hard at work from early morn until late at night.

But not all masters were cruel. Some were kind to their apprentices, took them on their travels and treated them as members of their own families.

The well trained apprentice made copies of his master's letters and kept simple accounts. He helped to pack and ship his master's cargoes. Sometimes he learned to speak other languages and to use foreign moneys.

After his apprenticeship of seven years he was called a journeyman and could then work for any master willing to hire his services.

Later, if he had saved sufficient money, he might start a business of his own.

The apprentice was dressed plainly in sober colours. His canvas or leather doublet had only one small ruff or collar. His strong breeches were of plain material and his cloak was lined with cotton. He wore a flat, woollen cap.

If apprentices broke the rules, they were punished and sometimes given a public whipping. If they were lazy, or refused to work, they were beaten and could be sent away from the town. Many then became rogues and vagabonds. But if they ran away from their masters, they were hunted down, and brought back.

They were entirely at the mercy of their masters. They received many a cuff or kick and were often underfed.

Copying the master's letters

SOME THINGS TO DO

1. Paint a picture of a night-watchman with his staff and lantern patrolling a deserted street. Underneath the picture write down what you imagine he is calling out.

2. Mime the following short scene without using words:—

   A night watchman walks down a dark street calling out the time and weather. He does not notice two footpads lurking in a passage. Shortly afterwards a group of travellers approach, accompanied by a link-boy with a lantern. Footpads attack the travellers, snatch their purses and dash off, leaving the travellers lying on the ground.

3. Make a chart like this and add any names you know which may have been formed from a craft or trade.

TRADE	NAME
John the Cooper	John Cooper
Tom the Smith	Tom Smith
--------------------	--------------------
--------------------	--------------------

4. Paint a picture of hawkers walking up and down a busy street calling their wares.

5. Paint a picture of a street fight between two gangs of apprentices.

6. Imagine you are an apprentice. Write a story of a day in your life.

Tell how you made copies of your master's letters, helped to pack some of his goods and watched them being loaded aboard a ship. Tell also how you went out in the evening, and the story of a fight between your band of apprentices and another group. You managed to get home just before curfew, but one of your friends was late. Say what happened to him the next morning.

glass seller

tobacco stall

knife grinder

WORK IN THE HOME

There was always plenty of work to do at home, both in town and country.

People in towns could buy some of the things they needed—food, cloth and tools—from merchants and craftsmen, or from farmers and pedlars at the markets and fairs. But not many folk could afford to buy everything they needed. Some of the towns-people still grew some of their food in gardens behind their houses or in the fields outside the old town walls.

In the country there were no shops. The farmer sometimes took his wife on horseback to the town market, if there was one nearby, and to the fair. But it was often a long, slow journey and they would be away from home for a whole day.

Sometimes a pedlar visited the village or called at the farmhouses.

This was a special event, and the women and girls gathered round him to choose from his stock of ribbons, laces, needles, combs and pieces of cloth and silks, and to hear the news of happenings in other places.

Most of the food and articles people needed, both in town and country, had to be grown or made at home. In the large houses there were many servants to do all the work and the master and mistress of the house kept a sharp eye on them. But in the smaller homes everyone had to help. The men and boys worked in the fields and cared for the animals. The women and girls were always busy cooking, spinning, weaving, making and mending clothes, and doing all the many jobs that had to be done in and around the house.

Pedlar showing his wares to country women and children

Milk was made into butter and cheese.

Bread, cakes, pies and pastries were baked in clay or brick ovens in the kitchen or an outdoor bakehouse.

First, wood was burned inside the oven. Then the ashes were raked out and the food was pushed inside on a long wooden shovel. It was cooked by the heat from the bricks.

Meat was boiled or stewed in large iron pots hanging on hooks and chains over the log fire. Or it was roasted on spits.

Kitchen activities

Dairying

There was plenty of work to do in the kitchen. Meat and fish had to be salted and pickled. Bacon and hams were cured and salted.

The women had to see that they had enough salt in the house, both for preserving and everyday use. It was kept in a special salt-box near the fire to keep it dry.

Large joints and small pigs were sometimes roasted in an iron cage fastened on a spit, called a cradle- or basket-spit.

In large houses the spit was sometimes turned by a boy called a 'turnspit'. Later, gears and weights were arranged to turn the spit automatically.

Fish and meat were also grilled on grid-irons.

Spit

49

Girls had to learn from their mothers how to make jams, marmalades and pickles, how to brew ale and beer, and make wines and syrups from fruits, plants and berries.

They had to learn how to do all the jobs in the house so they would be able to manage their own homes when they married.

They began to stitch and sew and make clothes while quite young. They practised their stitches on 'samplers' and then embroidered cushions, stool-covers, curtains and fire-screens with beautiful patterns.

Clothes were made at home with strong material that could be mended and patched again and again.

After the sheep were sheared, the wool was cleaned, carded, and dyed with dyes made from roots, berries, lichens and leaves. Then it was oiled, carded again and spun into thread on a spinning-wheel.

The women also spun linen thread from flax. The spinning-wheel was always in use, spinning woollen and linen thread for clothes, sheets, blankets, napkins and tablecloths.

Jacobean tapestry

Sometimes the thread was woven into cloth on a loom at home, but usually this was done by a travelling weaver.

16th century spinning wheel

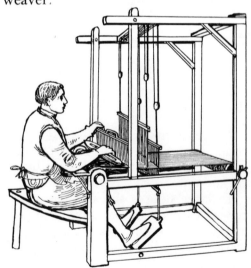

Weaving on a loom

50

Washing day

Rooms were lit by candles, rush-lights and sometimes by oil lamps.

Villagers could not afford many candles and so most of them used rush-lights. They gathered the rushes in summer, peeled off most of the skin, dried them and dipped them in melted cooking grease.

Candles could be bought from candlemakers, but many were made at home by dipping a cotton or rush wick several times into melted mutton fat until it had a thick wall of fat round it.

Some candles were made from beeswax, but these were expensive and were used only in churches and the houses of rich people.

The wick had to be trimmed or ' snuffed ' from time to time and this was done with ' snuffers ', like scissors.

Clothes were not washed very often, only about once every three months. The larger houses had a special room for the laundry, but in ordinary houses the washing was done in the kitchen or outside in the open. The clothes were beaten with wooden bats to knock out the dirt and then were taken to a drying room or thrown over bushes in the sun.

Soap was made at home, from a mixture of fats and ashes, and stored in barrels. Sometimes it was scented with herbs to make the clothes smell sweet.

People washed in bowls and buckets, and wealthy people bathed in wooden tubs in front of the fire.

Teeth were cleaned by rubbing them with a soft cloth. Some people used silver, gold or ivory tooth-picks.

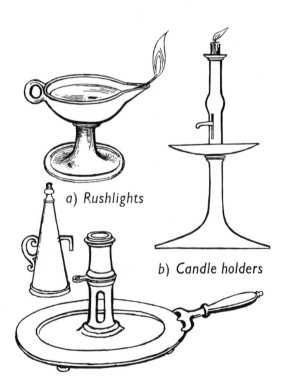

a) *Rushlights*

b) *Candle holders*

There were few doctors in those days and the mistress of the house cared for the sick. She collected plants and herbs and made medicines and ointments from them.

Some women made their own cosmetics—dyes for their hair, lotions for their hands, and scented water to remove freckles and wrinkles.

Pots, Pans and Tableware

There was plenty of work to do and a great many pots and pans to scour and clean.

In the poorer homes people used wooden plates, bowls and spoons, and drank their ale and beer from horn tumblers. Some still used thick slices of stale bread as plates.

But by now the richer farmers and tradesmen were using pewter and earthenware, and in the larger houses there were silver dishes and Venetian glasses.

Fruit and sweets were sometimes served on special dishes called ' roundels.' These were thin plates with a pattern and a rhyme on one side.

Soup and porridge were eaten from bowls called ' porringers.'

Food was still eaten with a knife, a spoon and fingers. Travellers to Italy had brought forks back with them, but people thought they were novelties. It was still fashionable to rinse fingers in a basin of water between each course.

sauce pan and skillet

coffee pot

Apostle spoon

bronze mortar and pestle

jug

Mazer Bowl

ladle : fork

Some kitchen utensils and tableware of the period

FOOD AND DRINK

People usually had two main meals a day—dinner at about eleven o'clock in the morning and supper about five or six o'clock in the evening.

Labourers and the poorer farmers had roast meat only once or twice a week. For the rest of the week they had to be content with pease or pottage with a lump of pork or bacon in it, fish, eggs, cheese, butter and churned milk. They drank their own home-brewed cider, ale and beer.

They often took their dinner with them to the fields, where they sat on the ground with their jug of beer, an apple pasty and hunks of bread and cheese.

Family at Dinner

Farmworkers eating in the fields

Workers in the towns ate more meat than the poor country labourers, and they had more varied meals with brawn, bacon, souse, fowls and fruit which they could buy from the shops and markets.

Most people, both in town and country, ate fresh or salt fish on fish days and during Lent. Town folk were able to buy it from the fishmonger when they needed it. But people in the country had to fish for it in rivers and ponds. After harvest the farmers had to ride into the nearest town and buy salt fish and herrings to store during the winter.

The majority of people ate coarse brown bread made from rye or barley. When times were hard and crops were poor, they had to make it from oats, peas or beans and sometimes from acorns. Only wealthy people ate white bread made with wheat flour.

Dinner in a wealthy household

In the houses of nobles, gentlemen and rich merchants, dinner often lasted two or three hours, especially if the master of the house had guests.

There was always a wide choice of dishes so the guests could choose something they liked from each course. The servants fed on what was left from the table.

There were usually several different joints of meat to choose from—roast beef, boiled salted beef, stuffed mutton, veal or venison.

The fish course might include pike, trout, salmon, eel, whiting or plaice, and there might be shell fish on the menu.

There were poultry dishes, salads, meat pies, vegetables, pasties, and many kinds of sweetmeats, fruits and home-made cheeses. There is no wonder that dinner lasted such a long time.

The diners drank home-made ale and beer or wine. The wine was kept cool in a tub of water. Each time a guest wanted a drink, his glass was rinsed in a wooden tub before it was refilled.

Most of the food was grown in the garden or in the countryside. But some things, such as pepper, sugar, cloves and ginger were sent from London to the towns and markets. These had been brought by sea from foreign lands.

SOME THINGS TO DO

1. Paint pictures of some jobs that were done in the home during Tudor and Stuart times.

   Paste your pictures on a frieze for the wall of the classroom.

   Write some sentences about each picture and paste them underneath.

2. Draw pictures of different kinds of tableware used in Tudor and Stuart times. Cut them out and paste them on a wall chart and label them.

3. Paint large pictures of:—
   a. People at dinner in a large house.
   b. Farm workers eating in the fields.
   c. Men fishing in a river.
   d. A farmer riding home from market with a basket of herrings.

Boy turnspit

4. Imagine you are one of the servants working in an Elizabethan mansion.

   Queen Elizabeth and her Court recently came to visit your master and mistress.

   Write or tell the story of the busy preparations for the visit, the arrival of the royal party, the banquet on the first night and the departure of the Queen.

WORK IN THE HOME IN TUDOR AND STUART TIMES

GAMES AND AMUSEMENTS

Boys and girls enjoyed many games that we still play today—hop-scotch, stool-ball, hide-and-seek, leap-frog and blind-man's-buff.

Hoops were bowled and tops whipped along the dusty tracks.

Kites flew over village greens and shuttle-cocks were knocked through the air.

Blind man's buff

Tennis and billiards were only played in the large houses, but there were many other games for both children and adults. Bowls was a popular game.

In "nine-holes" balls were rolled into holes in the ground or on a special board. People chose turns by "handy-dandy"; one person hid a small stone in his hand and the other had to guess which hand it was in.

Spinning tops

Shuttlecocks

Football was another favourite game, but there were no rules and no pitch as we have today. The ball was kicked round the houses, over the green, and up and down the lanes. It was very rough and players were often seriously injured. Wrestling was another rough game.

Bowls

Men played a game like golf, called 'bandy-bar'.

Others 'pitched the bar'. Each man, in turn, lifted a tree trunk from the ground. Holding it upright, he ran forward and tossed it through the air. The winner was the man who threw it the farthest.

In the country there was swimming, fishing, hunting, hawking and duck-shooting. Both men and boys practised archery and shot at targets with long bows and arrows.

Bandy bar

Bear baiting

Some of the sports were very cruel. Men and women flocked to see bull-baiting and bear-baiting. The bear was tied to a post by a long chain and then fierce dogs were set on it. The bear fought back until the dogs were killed or the bear was seriously injured. Then the fight was stopped.

People also went to cock-fighting. Two trained fighting cocks fought each other until one was killed or too injured to fight any longer.

There were, of course, the quieter indoor games of draughts, chess and backgammon. Young boys and girls also had pets, toy animals, rocking horses and dolls. In the evening and when the weather was bad, they sat indoors to play with their toys and listen to stories from mother and older sisters.

Hawking and hunting

Fairs were still held and people stared in wonder at the many side-shows, the jugglers, acrobats, fire-eaters and dancing bears. They shouted themselves hoarse watching wrestling matches, cudgel bouts and broadsword fights.

Dancing and acting were very popular. Lords and ladies danced in the long galleries and the villagers on the green or in their master's hall. The country folk enjoyed their gay jigs, hornpipes and morris dances.

There were no Bank Holidays, but people made merry whenever they could on church festivals or feast-days and at the important seasons of the year.

On May Day, men, women and children went out to the woods to gather branches and leaves. A tall, young tree was cut down for a Maypole and this was dragged back to the village green by twenty to forty oxen. Each ox had a nosegay of flowers tied to the tips of its horns. Then the pole was

The Maypole

covered with flowers and herbs; coloured strings were bound round it from top to bottom; it was set up with gay flags and handkerchiefs on top, and people spent the day feasting and dancing round it.

Scene at a fair

Morris dancers

Lord of misrule and attendants

On Plough Sunday the plough was taken to the village church to be blessed. On the next day the young men, dressed in white shirts, pulled the plough through the village. At each house they stopped to collect money for the feast. If anyone refused to give, the plough might be pulled over his garden.

The Elizabethans liked play-acting. In the country, mummers and travelling actors went from village to village—singing, dancing, miming and acting plays. In the town plays were acted in the courtyards of large inns. The players acted their story on a platform in the yard and people watched either from the floor of the yard or from the inn galleries.

Sometimes the young men chose a captain and called him the 'lord of misrule'. They dressed in brightly coloured clothes, with gay scarves, laces and ribbons, covered with rings and jewels. With twenty or more bells on each leg, they marched and danced through the village with hobby-horses, dragons, pipers and drummers.

With bells jingling and handkerchiefs waving, they danced through the church and back into the churchyard, where they spent the rest of the day—and sometimes the night—in feasting and dancing.

There were other festivals too—at Easter, Shrove Tuesday and Whitsuntide. Some villages had their own special feast-days when everyone made merry. Christmas was a time for holiday and rejoicing. At harvesttime, too, the workers feasted and danced in the master's hall or in one of his barns.

Play acting in an Inn yard

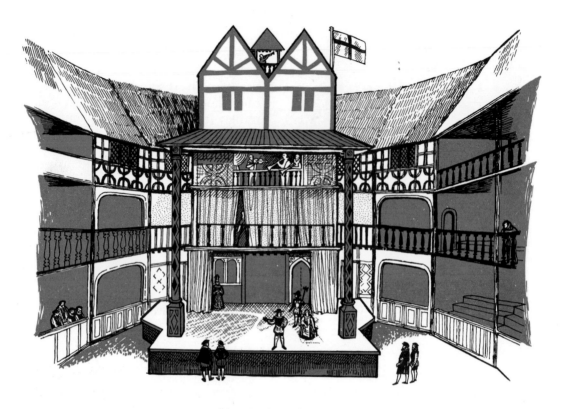

Elizabethan theatre

It was during Queen Elizabeth's reign that the first theatres were built in London. They were built of wood and looked very much like the inn yards.

In the middle was an open space with tiers of galleries round it. People stood in the open round the stage or sat in the galleries under cover.

Most of the play was acted on the huge platform which jutted out into the middle of the yard.

At the back, an opening with a curtain over it led to a smaller stage which was used for 'indoor' scenes. Above it was a balcony for parts of the play which had to be acted high up, such as the top of castle walls. Over this was the gallery where the musicians played.

In the floor of the stage there were 'traps' where dead bodies could be buried or ghosts could rise into the air.

Performances began at three o'clock in the afternoon. A trumpet was sounded from the turret on the roof to tell people that the play was about to begin and a flag was flown while the play was being acted.

There was no scenery and very little furniture. There were no women actresses; their parts were played by boys.

These theatres were very popular and crowds of people attended to watch plays like 'A Midsummer Night's Dream'.

The most famous plays were those written by William Shakespeare and by Christopher Marlowe.

SCHOOLS AND MUSIC

By the time of Elizabeth and the Stuarts, most towns had grammar schools for boys whose fathers could afford to pay the fees.

Before they went to school they learned to read at home from a horn book. This was like a wooden bat. A piece of paper with the alphabet and the Lord's Prayer written on it was stuck on the bat and covered with a piece of horn to protect it.

Boys went to the grammar schools when they were seven years old. The school hours lasted from six o'clock in the morning until eleven and then from one o'clock until five or six. The chief lessons were Latin, Greek and some Arithmetic. Some of the boys went on to the Universities at the very early age of fifteen.

Girls stayed at home and learned how to sew and cook and run the house. Only daughters of wealthy people learned how to read and write and speak foreign languages.

Every educated person was expected to be able to read music. People

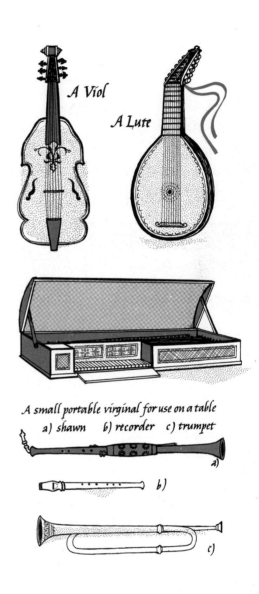

A Viol

A Lute

A small portable virginal for use on a table
a) shawm b) recorder c) trumpet

Horn book

entertained themselves by singing songs or playing musical instruments.

Indeed, they were so fond of music that barbers' shops often had a lute hanging on the wall so that customers could play while waiting for their turn.

SOME THINGS TO DO

1. Paint a picture of children playing each of the games shown on Page 56 and also any of the following: hide-and-seek, hop-scotch, bowling hoops, flying kites, and football. You can also draw pictures of children fishing, swimming and practising archery.

2. You have spent a day at the fair. Write a story telling how you went there, and what you saw and did. Describe some of the sideshows you saw, including the acrobats, jugglers and the bear baiting.

3. Write about:—
   a. May-day,
   b. Plough Monday,
   c. ' The Lord of Mis-rule.'

4. Paint a large picture of a play being acted on the stage of an Elizabethan theatre. Show people standing on the floor around the stage and others in the galleries. Remember the flag on the roof.

Wrestling

5. Find out from your class library all you can about William Shakespeare:—
   —where he was born,
   —where he went to school,
   —the names of some of his plays,
   —where his plays were performed in London.

6. Make a chart showing different musical instruments used in the days of the Tudors and Stuarts.

Guild Chapel Grammar School, Stratford on Avon

COSTUME

This noble lady of early Tudor times is wearing a gable hood and a long velvet gown. Her skirt has a long train fastened up to her waist and her girdle is richly embroidered.

a) Lady of Early Tudor times

This merchant's long gown is lined with fur. He is wearing wide, square-toed shoes.

b) Tudor merchant and son

c) Elizabethan gentlemen

Men of Elizabethan times wore a jerkin over a tunic called a doublet. Their trunk-hose were sometimes padded with horse-hair. They wore starched ruff collars.

This Elizabethan lady's full skirt is called a farthingale. It hangs over a petticoat which has been stiffened with hoops to make a framework. Her lace collar is called a ruff.

d) Elizabethan lady

Cavaliers

During the reign of Charles I some men wore leather boots with turned-down tops. Others wore shoes with large rosettes of ribbon. The ruff of Elizabethan days was replaced by a large lace collar. Men grew their hair long and often curled in ringlets. Many wore moustaches and small pointed beards. They sometimes wore ostrich plumes in their wide-brimmed hats.

As the farthingale went out of fashion, women's dresses became more graceful. Their full skirts, gathered at the waist, were worn over numerous petticoats. Women, too, began to wear lace collars instead of ruffs.

They seldom wore hats, except for riding or travelling, when they wore a plumed Cavalier hat made of velvet. At other times they often wore a silk scarf.

Ladies at the time of Charles I

The Puritans thought it wicked to wear brightly coloured clothes. Their own were plainly made of black, brown or grey material. Both men and women wore white linen collars and cuffs. Most Puritan women also wore a long, narrow, white apron. Men had their hair cut short and wore tall, black hats. Women wore similar hats, but often wore small white linen caps underneath.

Great changes took place in men's fashions about the time of Charles II. Doublets were gradually replaced by coats and waistcoats. Coats and breeches were often decorated with bows and loops of ribbon, satin and velvet. Men now wore a piece of linen, called a cravat, tied in a bow at the throat. Some wore wigs of curls which hung over the shoulders and down the back. Square shoes had flat, wide bows of ribbons or small, metal buckles.

Puritan man and woman

Women's fashions changed only slightly during Charles II's reign. Their dresses were tightly corsetted and had full skirts which hung in graceful folds to the ground. Sometimes the skirt was open at the front and fastened back to reveal a differently coloured petticoat underneath. Silk and satin were popular with the more wealthy women.

Fashions of the Restoration period

65

Late Stuart fashion

Towards the end of the Stuart period men's coats were longer and were usually left unbuttoned, or merely fastened at the waist. Men began to wear three-cornered hats called tricornes, though some preferred to carry them so that their wigs could be seen. A few powdered their wigs, some of which by this time reached almost to the waist.

Women wore a new style of farthingale known as the hoop. Their hair was arranged in curls and waves on top of the head. They wore a tall head-dress which was a little cap decorated in front with layers of lace and ribbons. Usually a silk scarf covered the back of the head like a hood.

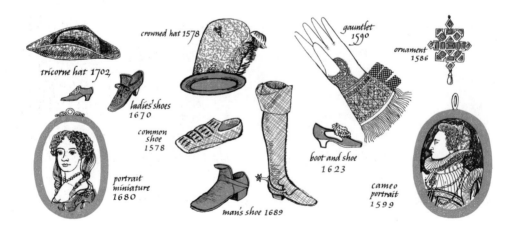

tricorne hat 1702

crowned hat 1578

ladies' shoes 1670

common shoe 1578

portrait miniature 1680

man's shoe 1689

boot and shoe 1623

gauntlet 1590

ornament 1586

cameo portrait 1599

SOME THINGS TO DO

1. Make some dolls using pipe-cleaners, or pieces of wire, or rolls of newspaper.

   Dress them with pieces of material as people of Tudor and Stuart times. The illustrations shown below and those on pages 63 to 66 will help you.

Countryman and country woman

2. Trace the figures shown in the illustrations on to cardboard. Paint them, cut them out and insert them in slotted corks. Write notes about each.
3. Make a large wall frieze. Draw a group of people from Tudor and Stuart times. You can either paint them or dress them by sticking pieces of material on the figures. Write their names on pieces of card and paste them on the frieze.
4. Make a theatre stage from a cardboard box. Put your cut-out figures on the stage to represent a scene from a play. Paint the scenery for the play on the inside of the box. Write the story of the play.
5. On a page of your notebook draw pictures of some of the hats, gloves, shoes and jewellery worn by the Tudors and Stuarts.

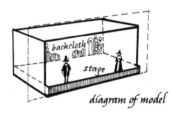

diagram of model

A Restoration Theatre Stage 1690

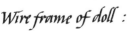

Wire frame of doll :   covering

STUART HOUSES

In the past, houses had been planned by the owner and the men who built them.

But in Stuart times large houses were designed by men called architects, who had studied buildings. These men had often travelled in other lands, especially in Italy. They used the ideas they had seen there to plan a new kind of English house.

These new houses were built in brick and stone, in the shape of a rectangle, with all the rooms under one roof.

They placed the doorway in the centre of the front, with an equal number of windows on each side. If a line was drawn down the centre of the house, each half was exactly alike. The house was symmetrical in design.

Everything was planned so that it was in correct proportion. Doors, windows, walls, rooms, ceilings, had to be the right size and shape so that everything fitted together and looked right.

The roof was ' hipped '—that is, it sloped back on all four sides.

The windows were flat and rectangular, like the front of the house. At first, they opened like casements. Later, ' sash ' windows were introduced. These were made in two parts. Each part slid up and down and stayed open in any position.

Coleshill, Berks.

17th century dining room

Jacobean carved stair-case

Inside the house, the rooms were large and high, with plastered and painted ceilings. Walls were panelled with richly carved wood. Oil paintings and portraits hung on the walls.

The hall was smaller and was now used as an entrance lobby with doors leading to drawing rooms and dining rooms.

A richly carved staircase, similar to the one shown, led to the upper floors and the bedrooms.

Surveyor supervising parish roadmaking

TRANSPORT

The Roads

Towards the end of the Middle Ages priests and monks had sometimes repaired many of the roads. But after Henry VIII closed the monasteries the roads were neglected.

By this time trade between towns was rapidly increasing and goods were being sent to the seaports for shipment overseas. Better roads were needed to cope with the traffic.

In 1555 the Highway Act ordered each parish to repair its own roads, and two men called surveyors were chosen each year to organize this work.

Every labourer in the parish was supposed to work for six days each year, but as they were unpaid, they worked very slowly and wasted time. Some tried to avoid the work by paying a fine or by finding someone else to do it for them.

Few surveyors, however, knew much about roadmaking and so the roads were not improved. Many were left with deep holes and ruts, which filled with water in wet weather. Few landowners kept an open strip of land on each side of the road, although that was the law.

Overhanging trees and bushes kept the roads wet and muddy, and the horses' hoofs and the heavy wheels of carts and wagons churned up the mud and made the roads even worse.

Most people travelled on horseback or else on foot. Travellers who did not own horses of their own could hire them from inns called posting-houses for a few pence per mile. About ten miles further along the road, the horses would be left at another inn and new horses hired for the next stage of the journey. Occasionally horses were stolen in spite of the fact that punishment for horse-stealing was death.

During the sixteenth century, stage-waggons began to run regular services between certain towns. These were long, lumbering, springless waggons, pulled by six or more horses. They carried goods and a few passengers, but had no seats, and passengers sat on the floor among the straw or bales of soft goods. The waggoner walked for most of the journey by the head of the leading horse. The law forbade him to drive his team of horses from aboard the waggon, in case he should fall asleep.

Only the poorer people travelled by stage-waggon, and the journey was slow and uncomfortable. At night the passengers could not afford to stay at an inn, so they often slept in a barn or hay-loft. Frequently they slept on the floor of the waggon.

As more and more traffic used the roads, they became worse and worse.

Pack horses

Instead of improving the roads, certain Acts of Parliament tried to prevent heavy traffic from using them. One Act, for example, stopped waggons and carts from carrying loads of more than a ton. Another ordered wheels to be at least four inches wide, for it was thought that wide wheels would help to roll out some of the ruts.

Long trains of packhorses still made their way along the muddy roads, carrying goods from town to town, and to the busy seaports.

An early stage-waggon

Stage coach arriving at an Inn

Coaches

Coaches were first used in this country about the time of Queen Elizabeth, although they had been used in France and Holland several years earlier.

These early coaches had no springs and the body of the coach rested on the axles. Naturally they were very uncomfortable as they jolted and bumped along the deeply rutted roads.

Only the richer people owned coaches, but they could be hired for journeys in and about London for ten shillings a day.

During the 17th century, coaches were made more comfortable by suspending the bodywork, first from leather straps, and then later from steel springs. By this time also, some coaches had glass windows.

About 1650, coaches began to make regular journeys across the country. Every ten or fifteen miles they stopped at an inn, or stage, to change horses or pick up passengers, and therefore became known as stage-coaches.

At first, stage-coaches ran only during the summer months, but later they ran throughout the year.

Some journeys lasted several days and, because of the bad roads, took much longer during the winter months than in summer. A journey from London to York sometimes took from four to eight days.

Each night the passengers stayed at one of the many inns along the roadside. Ordinary travellers ate their meals at a common table and slept on straw before the fire, but there were well-furnished, comfortable private rooms for those who could afford them.

Sometimes, servants at the inns were confederates of the many robbers and highwaymen who roamed the countryside. News of wealthy passengers was passed on to these rogues, who waited for the stage-coach as it continued its journey the following day.

Turnpikes and Tolls

In 1663 the first Turnpike Act was passed. This stated that money should be collected from travellers at certain points along the roads and spent on repairs. These payments were called tolls.

Tolls were first collected on a busy part of the old North Road, but were later collected every few miles along other main roads.

At first the roads were not blocked in any way, but sometimes travellers dashed past the collector without paying toll. So toll-bars were built and each had a pole or pike which could be put across the road.

After the toll had been paid, the pike was turned to allow travellers to pass.

People on foot, farm waggons, soldiers and postboys who carried the mails, were some of those who paid no tolls, but horses, coaches, carts, pigs, sheep and cattle were all charged at various rates.

Later, gates were used instead of poles and some had sharp spikes to prevent people on horseback from leaping over them. But the name turnpike remained and was later given to the main roads themselves.

The toll-keeper lived in a small house which was built beside the toll-gate.

Scene at a Toll gate

73

Ships

During Tudor and Stuart times sailing ships underwent great changes. Seamen were discovering new lands across the seas and stronger ships were needed for the long ocean voyages.

Men were becoming more skilled with tools and could now build ships with smooth sides. These ships were longer and more slender, and could travel much faster than the earlier broad ships.

Ships normally had three masts. The foremast and the mainmast each carried a square sail, but that on the mizzen mast was called a lateen sail. Above the square sails were others called topsails. Another sail was sometimes carried under the bowsprit.

The front of the ship was still called the forecastle, though it no longer looked much like a castle. The remainder of the ship was made up of

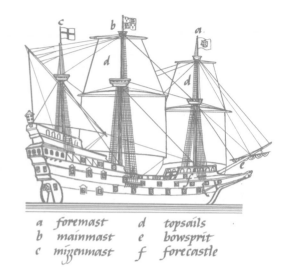

a	foremast	d	topsails
b	mainmast	e	bowsprit
c	mizzenmast	f	forecastle

Tudor ship

three decks. The lowest was called the main deck, next came the quarter deck, and above this was the poop-deck where the captain had his quarters.

Nearly all merchant ships were armed with cannon, not only to defend themselves against attack from pirates, but also in case they were needed as warships. Henry VIII built several large warships.

The most famous was named ' Henri Grace à Dieu,' but some people called it Great Harry.

At first cannon were fired from the deckside, but later they were placed on lower decks and fired through portholes. The gunners could fire in greater safety from there.

The new style of firing broadsides from cannon at the sides of the ship was a big improvement. Previously, ships had tried to ram each other so that the soldiers aboard could grapple with the enemy.

Henri Grâce à Dieu

Living conditions at sea

During Stuart times the middle of the ship had an upper deck above the main deck. Later ships were beautifully carved and gilded at the bows and stern. One such ship was the "Sovereign of the Seas", which was built for King Charles I. At that time she was the largest ship ever built.

Although the captain and his officers had richly furnished cabins, the seamen had a very hard life, with uncomfortable conditions and poor food.

Their cramped quarters were in the forecastle of the ship, which was often damp and smelly. Sometimes there was hardly room to lie down, though hammocks began to be used during the reign of Queen Elizabeth.

The men lived on dried and salted meat or fish, biscuits, butter and cheese, but much of the food soon went bad. They had no fresh vegetables or fruit while at sea and so they often caught a skin disease called scurvy. The main drink was beer, as fresh water soon became stale at sea.

Many seamen were rough and brutal and only the hardiest survived the many long ocean voyages. Hunger, sickness, shipwreck and piracy were some of the many hazards risked by seamen of Tudor and Stuart times.

SOME THINGS TO DO

1. A merchant was travelling home from London when his horse went lame. He had to hire the only horse that was left at the next posting-house.

   Tell the story of what happened to him before he reached home.

2. Paint large pictures of:—

   a. A scene on the road showing an early stage waggon and a train of packhorses.

   b. A stage-coach on a winter journey.

   c. A horseman leaping over the toll-gates.

3. Imagine you are a waggoner who has just returned home after a long journey. Tell your family about the people who travelled with you; the amusing incidents that occurred when the waggon wheels slipped into a deep rut; how they were eventually pulled out; what

Stage coach hold-up

happened to the man who spent the night in the waggon.

4. Write the story of a journey by stage-coach from London to York.

   Describe the passengers on the coach, a night at an inn and a hold-up by highwaymen.

   Draw pictures to illustrate your story.

Merchant at post house exchanging horses

SEAMEN, EXPLORERS AND SETTLERS

Early Discoveries

During the Middle Ages men had brought spices to the countries of Europe from India and the East. But after the Turks conquered Egypt, Palestine and Syria, it became difficult for merchants to make their long journeys over land. The Turks demanded payment from all who carried goods across their countries. Often, too, travellers were attacked and robbed of their valuable possessions.

So men began to seek other routes to the East and to explore the seas.

Bartholomew Diaz

In 1486 a Portuguese seaman called Bartholomew Diaz sailed round the southern tip of Africa. He named it the Cape of Storms because of the bad weather he found there. Later, the King of Portugal renamed it the Cape of Good Hope, for the sea-route to India was now clear.

Diaz, however, returned home, for his store of food was low and his crew were reluctant to venture further.

Vasco da Gama

Twelve years later another Portuguese seaman, Vasco da Gama, also sailed round the Cape of Good Hope. After a voyage of almost a year he reached India. Soon afterwards the Portuguese were sailing regularly to India.

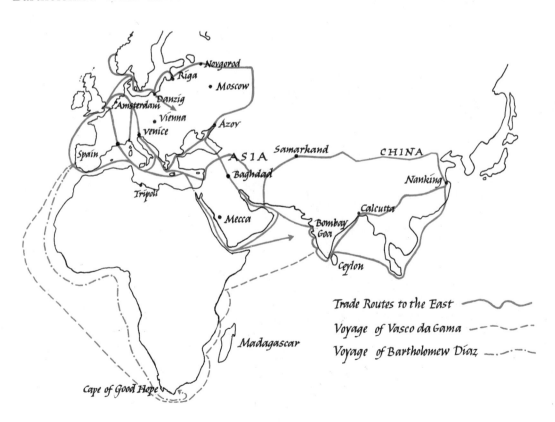

Trade Routes to the East

Voyage of Vasco da Gama

Voyage of Bartholomew Diaz

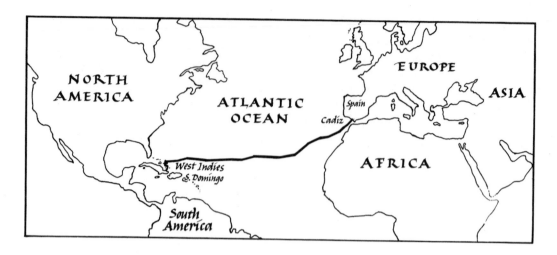

The first Voyage
of COLUMBUS

Christopher Columbus

Some years earlier an Italian seaman, Christopher Columbus, had attempted to reach India by another route.

Columbus was convinced he could reach India by sailing westwards, and he persuaded the King of Spain to give him three ships for the voyage. These were called the 'Santa Maria', the 'Nina' and the 'Pinta.'

In August 1492 Columbus sailed westwards in search of India. But his crews were nervous of sailing where no man had ever sailed before. In those days seamen thought that the earth was flat and were afraid they might sail over the edge.

As the voyage continued and no land came in sight, they became mutinous. Eventually, after a voyage of almost two months, land was at last sighted. Columbus was certain he had reached India, but it was one of a group of islands near the coast of America. Because of his mistake we still call these islands the West Indies.

Later, Columbus discovered other lands on the coast of South America. This made Spain one of the richest countries in the world, for the lands of South America contained gold and silver mines.

Columbus asking the King of Spain for help

Ferdinand Magellan

In 1519 Ferdinand Magellan, another Portuguese seaman, sailed with five ships across the Atlantic Ocean from Seville in Spain. He also hoped to discover another route to India and the East.

Magellan sailed down the Atlantic coast of South America searching for a way through the great continent. After many months some of his officers and crews wanted to return. One of his ships turned for home and another was lost.

When Magellan discovered some of his men were plotting to murder him, he landed and hanged the ringleader of the mutineers. He then continued on his voyage.

Eventually Magellan found a narrow passage between the southern tip of South America and a group of islands. After a hazardous voyage through fogs and storms, he sailed through this rocky sea passage, (now known as the Magellan Straits), into the Pacific Ocean.

For 98 days Magellan and his crew sailed across this vast unknown ocean with no sight of land. Many of his crew were dying of hunger and thirst.

At last he arrived at the Philippine Islands. Previous explorers had reached here by sailing eastwards. Magellan had done so by travelling westwards. This showed that the world was round.

He then intended to continue his journey homewards, but unfortunately he was killed in a battle between natives of two of the islands.

Magellan's crew in an exhausted condition, sailing across the Pacific

English ships attacking Spanish treasure ships

Another officer took command of the expedition and set off for home with the remainder of the crew in the one ship that remained seaworthy.

Eventually, after rounding the Cape of Good Hope, they arrived back at Seville. Although 280 men had set out three years previously, only 31 returned safely. These were the first men ever to sail round the world.

Discoveries for England

English seamen also began to sail across the Atlantic to the West Indies and the coasts of North and South America. Sometimes they went to trade with the people who lived there. But more often they attacked and robbed Spanish ships returning home laden with treasure.

John Cabot

In 1497 John Cabot had tried to find another way to India and the East by sailing westwards. Although he was not successful, he discovered Newfoundland and claimed it for England.

On a later voyage he sailed on further and explored the east coast of North America.

Some years later, during the reign of Queen Elizabeth I, many brave men sailed on voyages of discovery.

They left our shores, sometimes with their ships laden with English goods, and brought back rare cargoes from strange new lands.

Sir John Hawkins

In those days it was not considered cruel to buy and sell human beings as slaves.

One of the Englishmen who took part in slave trading was Sir John Hawkins. Hawkins sailed to the West coast of Africa, where he bought or captured negroes. He took them across the Atlantic and sold them to the Spaniards, although it was against the law for Spaniards to trade with foreigners. In exchange for the negroes Hawkins received gold, pearls and sugar.

The Spaniards made the negroes work as slaves on the sugar plantations of the West Indies, or in the gold and silver mines of South America.

Hawkins made two successful voyages of this nature, but on the third occasion, while anchored in a Spanish harbour, his ships were attacked by the treacherous Spaniards.

Although several of his ships were destroyed, Hawkins managed to escape and return to England with the remainder.

After this, there was no further peaceful trading with the Spaniards, and more and more English seamen raided the Spanish treasure ships.

Hawkins selling slaves to the Spaniards

L.H. 3—F

Sir Francis Drake

One of the most famous English seamen during the reign of Queen Elizabeth I was Sir Francis Drake. As a young man he had served under Sir John Hawkins. Later, he had commanded one of the ships that returned from Hawkins's third voyage.

Following this, Drake led a series of raids on the American coasts. In 1573 he attacked and robbed a Spanish mule train carrying silver across the narrow strip of Panama. Drake returned to his native Plymouth with his ship laden with silver worth about £20,000.

Four years later, he set out westward again with five ships on another treasure hunt. This time it was rumoured he had received secret instructions from Queen Elizabeth to enter the Pacific and attack the Spanish ships there.

Golden Hind

Sir Francis Drake

On the way some of his crews became discontented and rebellious. The leader of the rebels was a ship's officer called Thomas Doughty. Drake brought Doughty to trial, and after a jury had found him guilty of treason, he was sentenced to death and executed. By a strange coincidence he was beheaded in the very same place where Magellan's rebellious ringleader had been put to death over fifty years earlier.

After this, Drake had no more trouble with his men. He reduced his fleet to three fighting ships, renamed his own ship ' The Golden Hind ' and sailed through the Magellan Straits into the Pacific. Soon afterwards a violent gale sprang up and the three ships were separated. One, ' The Marigold,' disappeared and was never seen again. Another, ' The Elizabeth,' made its own way back to England, but Drake and the 'Golden Hind' continued on their voyage.

Golden Hind on the rocks

For several months Drake sailed along the Pacific coast of South America. He attacked and destroyed many Spanish ships and captured vast amounts of gold and silver. The unsuspecting Spaniards did not expect to find an English ship in the Pacific Ocean.

Drake then sailed northwards and landed on the coast of California as his ship was now leaking badly. He named his landing place New Albion and claimed it for Queen Elizabeth.

After his ship had been repaired, Drake set sail across the Pacific until he reached the Spice Islands. There he made an agreement with the Sultan that England should have the right to trade with the islands, and brought away six tons of cloves.

Drake continued his voyage across the Indian Ocean where the Golden Hind ran on to submerged rocks.

Drake ordered his crew to throw overboard some of the ship's heavy guns, stores, and even half the cargo of cloves, before the ship slowly slid off the rocks.

Drake trading in the Spice Islands

Drake then sailed homewards round the Cape of Good Hope and, on the 26th September, 1580, he re-entered Plymouth harbour. He was the first Englishman to sail round the world, and his journey had taken him nearly three years.

The Queen summoned Drake to her Court to hear the story of his adventurous voyage. Later, she knighted him aboard the 'Golden Hind.' Sir Francis Drake became a national hero.

Drake set out on further adventures. He raided the Spanish ports robbing and plundering wherever his men landed ashore.

King Philip decided that England must be conquered. He gathered together a fleet of about eighty ships at Cadiz harbour in the south of Spain.

Drake set sail for Cadiz with a fleet of twenty-three ships. He sailed right

Queen Elizabeth knights Drake

into the harbour and destroyed most of the larger Spanish ships.

Queen Elizabeth, hoping to avoid war with Spain, sent an apology to King Philip for Drake's action. But Philip's mind was determined and the following year he was again ready to attack England.

Drake's raid on Cadiz

*Lookouts light warning beacons as the
Armada is sighted*

The Defeat of the Spanish Armada

The King of Spain gathered together another large fleet of 150 ships. About 50 of these were heavily armed fighting ships, while the others carried stores, supplies and soldiers.

In July, 1588, this great fleet, or armada, as it was called, set sail for England. The Spaniards planned to sail up the English Channel to the Netherlands. There they intended to take aboard another 20,000 soldiers and land them on the southern coast of England.

Look-outs on the English coast sighted the approach of the Spanish Armada as it slowly sailed up the Channel. Beacon fires spread the alarm from hill to hill.

Piles of blazing wood sent the warning signal across the countryside and men prepared to defend their homes against the Spanish invaders.

English ships sailed out from Plymouth to attack the Spanish fleet. In command was Lord Howard, and with him were Drake, Frobisher and Hawkins.

Fierce battles were fought off the Isle of Wight. Despite some damage to its ships, the Spanish Armada continued on its way.

Meanwhile, more and more ships hastened to join the English fleet, which again attacked the Armada. More of the heavy galleons were damaged and the Spanish ships made for the French coast, where they anchored off Calais.

The English tried to drive the enemy ships on to sandbanks where they would be wrecked. However, the wind changed and the damaged Spanish fleet was able to escape to the open sea.

The crippled Spanish Armada fled northwards before the wind. Its leaking ships with broken masts and tattered sails were laden with sick and wounded men, and food and water supplies were running low.

To return to Spain they had to sail round the North of Scotland. There they ran into rough gales, and many of their ships were wrecked on the rocky coasts. Less than half of the once proud Spanish fleet returned home safely.

English fire ships create havoc in the Spanish fleet

During the night, eight old English ships, laden with wood, barrels of tar and gunpowder, moved silently towards the Spanish fleet as it lay at anchor. At a given signal they were set alight and the blazing vessels floated among the closely packed Spanish fleet, which scattered to avoid damage.

The English promptly attacked and another fierce battle followed. The Spanish ships were big and slow and rather like floating castles. The Spaniards tried to grapple with the English ships so that their soldiers could clamber aboard and capture them.

The English ships had an advantage because they were smaller and faster and had more guns. The battle lasted for eight hours, during which time several galleons were sunk and thousands of Spaniards were killed.

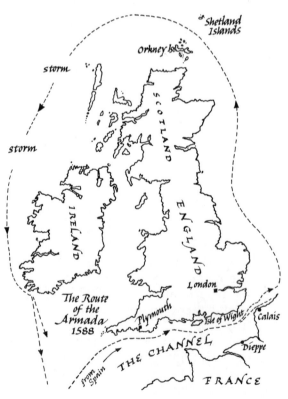

The route of the Armada

Early Colonies

Meanwhile, other seamen had continued their voyages of exploration. Some tried to start colonies of English people abroad, where they could settle and make new homes. Sometimes these were people who had been unable to find work in England. Others were men and women who had not been allowed to worship God as they wished.

These first attempts to start colonies were unsuccessful. Sometimes the natives were hostile and killed the strangers who came to their shores. Other settlers were unable to find food and died of starvation.

Sir Humphrey Gilbert attempted to start a colony in Newfoundland, but was not successful.

Sir Walter Raleigh tried to found a colony in Virginia and brought potatoes and tobacco back to this country. Raleigh was also a writer and a poet, and at one time was a great favourite of Queen Elizabeth. Later, however, he displeased the Queen, who had him imprisoned in the Tower, though he

Drake pow-wowing with Indians

was eventually released. In the reign of James I he was again thrown into the Tower and this time he was beheaded.

Colonists fighting off an Indian attack

Pilgrim Fathers sailing from Plymouth harbour

Later Settlers

During the 17th century more people sailed across the Atlantic and attempted to start new colonies. Like those who had sailed during Tudor times, most of them suffered great hardships. Some died of starvation, others of disease, while those who had expected to find gold were disappointed and often unwilling to work. Other settlers came from England to join them and new colonies were gradually developed.

Workers were needed for the large tobacco plantations in Virginia, and convicts and unemployed were sent out from England, Scotland and Ireland.

During the reign of James I the Puritans were not allowed to worship God in the way they wished. In 1620, some of them, together with their wives and families, left England and sailed for America in the 'Mayflower.' After a stormy voyage they reached the shores of North America. Their first task was to build themselves huts in which to live, and the women and children stayed aboard the 'Mayflower' until this had been done.

These Puritan settlers became known as the Pilgrim Fathers. They worked very hard to produce crops for themselves and later traded with the Indians.

Early
British Colonies
in N. America

Eventually they built themselves a town, which they called New Plymouth. More families crossed the Atlantic to join them, while others broke away to form separate colonies.

Meanwhile, in 1600, some London merchants had formed the English East India Company.

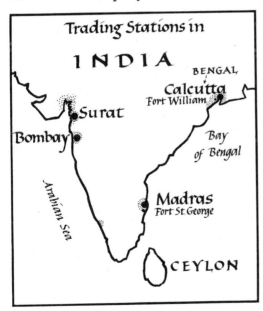

Trading Stations in
INDIA

They built special ships to carry cargoes of goods to India and the East. These cargoes they traded in exchange for articles that were in great demand in England.

Although these merchants made attempts to trade with the East Indies, the Dutch would not allow them to do so. After several battles with the Dutch fleet, the English merchants traded mainly with India.

Soon the merchants needed warehouses in which to store their goods. They made treaties with the Indian princes to set up trading stations at Surat, Bombay, Madras and Calcutta.

Because India was already thickly populated and had an unsuitable climate, the British did not form colonies of settlers there, as they did in America.

A trading station in India

89

SOLDIERS, ARMOUR AND WEAPONS

During early Tudor times a small regular army was formed by Henry VII. Its soldiers were called the Yeomen of the Guard.

In time of war, however, each village had to supply a number of soldiers, weapons and pieces of armour. There was no special uniform for these men and at first most of them wore a leather jerkin. Later, some wore suits of armour. Every fit man was supposed to have weapons ready for an emergency and be able to use them.

Although gunpowder had been used towards the end of the Middle Ages, the longbow was still the most common weapon. It could be fired quickly and with deadly accuracy. The bow was six feet long and was usually made of yew. The arrows, which were about three feet in length, had a heavy steel point and were feathered with goose feathers. The archer wore a leather guard on his wrist to protect it from the slap of the bow string.

During the Middle Ages cannon had been dangerous to use, for they often exploded when fired. During Tudor times they became heavier and less dangerous to fire, but they were mainly used for land sieges and sea battles.

Yeoman of Guard 1558

halberdier 1580

longbowman 1520

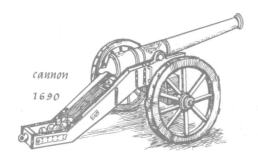

cannon 1690

plug bayonet attached to the musket

The cannon led to the invention of hand firearms. Early guns, such as muskets, arquebus and matchlocks, were heavy, and soldiers carried a forked stick on which to rest them when firing. These weapons could only be fired slowly, and in wet weather the rain often spoiled the gunpowder. Later, however, guns could be fired more quickly and with greater accuracy.

In the past it had taken a long while for an archer to become a skilled longbowman. Now men could be quickly trained to use firearms. So gradually the longbow was replaced by the musket.

As guns became more accurate, the risk of being hit by a bullet became greater. Armourers began to make thicker suits of armour to give greater protection. But heavy armour was uncomfortable to wear, and many foot-soldiers began to wear only the lighter pieces.

They preferred to risk being hit by a bullet rather than wear such clumsy, heavy armour. Most soldiers, nevertheless, still wore a breastplate, a backplate and a helmet.

Pikemen continued to wear armour until after the Civil War between the Roundheads and Cavaliers. They carried long pikes, or spears, and guarded the musketeers while they were reloading their weapons.

By this time the musket had been fitted with a bayonet. When the musketeer ran out of ammunition, his firearm could still be a useful weapon.

At first, the bayonet was a dagger that was pushed down the barrel of the empty musket, but later it was fitted round the outside of the barrel.

91

SOME THINGS TO DO

1. Draw a map to show the voyages of:—
   a. *Bartholomew Diaz,*
   b. *Vasco da Gama,*
   c. *Christopher Columbus,*
   d. *Ferdinand Magellan.*
2. Imagine you are a seaman who sailed round the world with Francis Drake. Tell the story of your adventures.
3. Paint large pictures of:—
   a. The 'Santa Maria' being loaded in harbour for her voyage. Show the busy scene on the dockside.
   b. Negroes working as slaves on the sugar plantations.
   c. The 'Golden Hind' in a storm at sea.
   d. Early settlers building their houses.

wheel lock pistol (twin barrelled) 1610

flintlock pistol 1680
powder flask

measured powder charge

plug bayonet

pike heads

rapier 1630

Hawkins's ships being attacked in a Spanish harbour

4. Make a book called 'Famous Elizabethan Seamen.' Write a chapter about each one and illustrate it.
5. Make a large wall-frieze of the Battle of the Armada.
6. Make up a play about Drake's voyage round the world:—
   Scene 1. The voyage begins. Goods are loaded on board and Drake's friends bid him farewell.
   Scene 2. Mutiny on board. Doughty is tried and executed.
   Scene 3. A storm at sea. The ship runs on rocks and the cargo is thrown overboard.
   Scene 4. At the Queen's Court. Drake tells the Queen the story of his adventures.
   Scene 5. Drake is knighted by the Queen aboard the 'Golden Hind.'
7. Paint a large picture of a battle between the Roundheads and the Cavaliers.

SOME FAMOUS PEOPLE

SAMUEL PEPYS

Samuel Pepys, who was born in 1633, was the son of a London tailor.

He held an important position at the Admiralty and became a Member of Parliament. He joined the Royal Society, a group of scientists and scholars which included Robert Boyle, Isaac Newton and Christopher Wren.

Pepys was most famous, however, for his diaries, which cover a period of nine years. He began to write these in a form of shorthand when he was 27.

From them we learn that he was fond of the theatre, liked to sing and could play several musical instruments.

In his diaries Pepys describes the clothes that people wore, the food they ate and the things he saw and heard as he walked about the streets of London.

At the time of the Plague, he tells how he saw two or three houses in Drury Lane marked with a red cross, and the words, ' Lord, have mercy upon us,' written on the doors.

Samuel Pepys

Pepys made sure he would not lose his precious notebooks in the Great Fire. He packed them with some of his other special possessions and sent them away to a friend in the country, where they would be safe.

His diaries give us a vivid and colourful description of life in London at that time.

He died in 1703.

Pepys, his wife and some friends making music at home

Purcell at the Westminster Abbey Organ.

JOHN MILTON

John Milton was a great English poet. His father lost his lands in Oxfordshire because he was a Protestant, and moved to London, where Milton was born in 1608. However, his father was able to give him a good education and at 16 John went to Cambridge University.

After leaving the university Milton wrote some of his famous poems and then travelled abroad, mostly in Italy. Later he returned and supported the side of Parliament against the King in the Civil War.

Afterwards, under Oliver Cromwell's rule, Milton was given an important government post. His eyesight had been failing for some time and in 1651 he became totally blind. However, Milton finished his great work 'Paradise Lost', and then wrote 'Paradise Regained.'

He died in 1674.

HENRY PURCELL (1659 - 1695)

Henry Purcell was a great musician. As a young boy he was a chorister at the Chapel Royal, which was the King's private chapel.

He became one of the King's composers at the age of 18, and by the time he was 20 he was organist at Westminster Abbey. Purcell wrote many anthems and songs, and composed music for the theatre.

He died at the age of 36 and was buried in Westminster Abbey.

Milton dictating to his secretary

ISAAC NEWTON

Isaac Newton was a famous mathematician and physicist who was born on Christmas Day, 1642. He studied mathematics at Cambridge University. While still a young man, he made several important scientific discoveries about mathematics, the different colours that make up white light, and the laws of gravity.

There is a story that one day, while Newton was sitting in his garden, he saw an apple fall from a tree. He began to wonder why an apple always fell downwards in a straight line to the ground. This started him thinking more about gravity, or the pull of the earth, and led him to important discoveries about the movements of the planets around the sun and the way in which the moon affects the tides.

Newton also made his own telescope

Newton and his telescope

and a copy of this is held by the Royal Society.

Later, he became Master of the Mint and the President of the Royal Society, and was knighted by Queen Anne.

In later years poor health forced him to give up his scientific work. He died when he was 84 and was buried in Westminster Abbey.

Newton in his garden

William Shakespeare — English dramatist poet & playwright

Sir Christopher Wren — Architect of St Paul's Cathedral, London

John Bunyan author of The Pilgrim's Progress

Guy Fawkes, conspirator and the Gunpowder Plot 1605

John Cabot — discoverer of Newfoundland 1497

Mary, Queen of Scots

Printed in Great Britain by Banks & Co. Ltd., Edinburgh